T0196634

HOW TO EDUCATE YOUR CHILDREN

in the 21st Century

Clynie Huggins

authorHOUSE

AuthorHouse™
1663 Liberty Drive
Bloomington, IN 47403
www.authorhouse.com
Phone: 1 (800) 839-8640

© 2019 Clynie Huggins. All rights reserved.

No part of this book may be reproduced, stored in a retrieval system, or transmitted by any means without the written permission of the author.

Published by AuthorHouse 11/04/2019

ISBN: 978-1-5462-7113-0 (sc)
ISBN: 978-1-5462-7112-3 (hc)
ISBN: 978-1-5462-7111-6 (e)

Library of Congress Control Number: 2018914271

Print information available on the last page.

Any people depicted in stock imagery provided by Getty Images are models, and such images are being used for illustrative purposes only. Certain stock imagery © Getty Images.

This book is printed on acid-free paper.

Because of the dynamic nature of the Internet, any web addresses or links contained in this book may have changed since publication and may no longer be valid. The views expressed in this work are solely those of the author and do not necessarily reflect the views of the publisher, and the publisher hereby disclaims any responsibility for them.

I am dedicating this book in the memory of my parents, O'neil and Edna Armstrong.

I am also dedicating this book to my family and friends.

Contents

Introduction

I wrote *How to Educate Your Children in the Twenty-First Century* to make parents aware of how to help their children receive a great education.

Education must start at home, with parents guiding their children through all stages of their development. This means setting goals for your child and then making sure that those goals are carried out. This also means making great choices in the selection of schools, beginning with day care (if used), preschool, and continuing through the twelfth grade. Making the best choice according to your child's needs of the school he or she will attend is of great importance. Children need to be guided in the direction in which they will be most successful.

After you find the school that will benefit your child and that offers the quality of education that will help your child be victorious, then enroll your child, help, and monitor your child's progress at that school.

Another significant aspect of education is your child's happiness and contentment. As parents, we desire our children to be comfortable at their schools so that learning will be exciting and more meaningful. You should begin goal setting for your child in the early months of pregnancy. From then until the baby is born, put goals and plans in place. Goal setting and planning should continue at birth on through elementary and secondary school. Goals also should be made for attending a higher level of education after finishing high school, such as a college, university, junior college, or trade school.

In this book I'll do the following:

- Outline the stages of child development, including language development
- Examine the types of childcare and the importance of finding an outstanding day care facility, if needed.
- Analyze, in detail, the two most popular childhood disorders, including common symptoms.
- Interpret educational foundations and rules for children, as these are an essential part of education
- Comment on the different types of schools
- Outline and explain the parent guide on what to look for in a good school and examine some school safety rules

By setting goals for your child, depending on the child's interests and abilities, you can make an intelligent choice of a school that will benefit his or her education. As parents, grandparents, administrators, and teachers, we should want the best for all children, as should the schools and the business community. Preparing for a great education will ensure this will happen. The school and business community should work toward helping schools in any way necessary to provide excellence in education. The community and businesses in the community of a school can make great contributions to a school. An example would be, a business could fund a computer program for the neighborhood school. Also, the citizens in the community can contribute by doing volunteer work at the community school as well as raise money for needed school supplies for the students at the community school. Public Schools also get help from the federal government, as well as the state and local government. Our children of today are our future for tomorrow.

This book is for parents of children of any age, as well as for anyone who is thinking of becoming a parent.

Chapter 1

Definition of Education

Education is the act or process of acquiring knowledge to develop understanding and judgment to be used in many areas of life. Education is a lifeline to a quality life. Because education is seen as the key to success, it should be effective, efficient, powerful, and adequate. If success depends upon education, then parents should want the best and most effective quality of education possible for their children. They should lead and guide their children effectively to meet the changes and challenges in schools, the community, and this society.

In the early history of education in America, dramatic changes took place rapidly.

Early History

American public education differs from education in many other countries. Education came into existence in the sixteen and seventeen hundreds. Although our education system began in earlier centuries, Thomas Jefferson was noted as one of the first government officials to support the public school system in the nineteenth century. Thomas Jefferson was a very smart man that believed in learning. He became the third president of the United States from March 4th, 1801 through March 4th 1809.

American public schooling came into existence in the 1600s in the New England colonies of Massachusetts, Connecticut, and New Hampshire. Its roots were derived from the Puritan and congregational religious schools. In 1779, Jefferson proposed a system of public education to be taxed and funded for three years for all the free children. Later Jefferson changed his ideas around, about who was free and worked toward education for all children. Thomas Jefferson was the governor of Virginia during the years of 1779 through 1781. Thomas Jefferson was an advocate of education and believed that children should be educated. During the time after the signing of the Declaration of Independence in 1776, other schools developed, including private and religious.

Until 1840, the education system was primarily for the wealthy. Reformers complained that this system was unjust and that education should be for all people. As a result of efforts to change the system, free public education at the elementary school level became available by the beginning of the 1900s. By 1918, all states had passed laws that children must attend school at the elementary level.

The Boston Latin School, founded in 1635, was the first secondary school. American high schools came into existence around 1751. Harvard was the first university at this time. The Morrill Acts of 1862 and 1890 provided federal funds to finance and support state universities. More students enrolled and became productive by attending and graduating from these universities.

Involvement at the Local, State, and Federal Levels

In the United States, public education is controlled by school districts within each state, and each state has an education administration department. Financing for public schools relies heavily on property taxes and from donations within the district from big business. The federal government also takes part, as it has the responsibility for funding the school programs that enhance the schools' regular programs. These federally funded programs provide effective education for students in public schools. One example of a federally funded program is, "The Early Childhood Development

Program." This program helps improve readiness and improved learning outcomes. This program helps to improve the knowledge and skills of early childhood educators. Other examples of federal programs in the United States that help public schools are the National School Lunch Program, No Child Left Behind Title I Grants, Head Start Program, IDEA Special Education Grants, and Youth Build Program.

During the 1980s and 1990s, school districts in the United States gave specific attention to raising educational standards. Academic tests were administered to public-school students to test their abilities in each subject in order to compare them on the local, state, and national levels. The school districts, schools, and teachers were pressured to help their students perform well with excellent scores on these tests. This expectation (or demand) that students produce excellent test scores continues today. States demand that students perform well on these tests. As a result of students performing poorly, drastic changes have occurred, such as teachers losing their jobs, losing needed school programs, and neighborhood schools closing. All of these changes have taken place in hope that students will improve the statistics of the past that have threatened the future of our public school system. The future of students performing poorly on these standardized tests, future could be affected because of reasons mentioned above. The public wants our schools to produce productive and efficient students who will set the pace for growth and development, also future economics. This country is in need of school districts that use effective programs that can help students grow and build powerful learning foundations in education. I think there should be more educational involvement between individual school boards, parents, administrators, and teachers.

Racial Equality

The first blacks arrived in this country in 1619. By the middle of the 1900s, there were 4.5 million black individuals in this country. The earliest education that they received was missionaries trying to convert them to Christianity. The southern states opposed the education of blacks. In 1863, Abraham Lincoln issued the Emancipation Proclamation. The literacy rate for black Americans went from 5 percent in the 1860s to 40 percent in 1890s and 70 percent by 1910.

In 1954, the US Supreme Court ruled in *Brown v. Board of Education of Topeka* that racial segregation in public schools was unconstitutional. By 1980, the federal courts had succeeded in eliminating the system of legalized segregation in Southern schools.

Clynie Huggins

Gender Equality

Women in early history did not have rights as the men had. Women and girls were discriminated against in public schools. Excellent women educators were Catherine Esther Beecher, Emma Willard, Jane Addams, Susan Anthony, and Mary McLeod. They established higher levels of learning for women. The women's rights movement during the 1960s brought about a change in public education. Title IX of the 1972 federal education amendment prohibited educational discrimination on the basis of sex.

Chapter 2

Educational Goals and Outcomes of America

egislation in the 1900s stated that every child in America would get a quality education. In this twenty-first century, one of the main goals is to produce intelligent and productive students who can compete, produce, and create through effective education.

Parents' Goals for Their Children

After you learn the sex of your unborn baby, choose several names, and then pick from the list of names. Some parents pick names that stand for different things, such as Love, Diamond, Prince, or Princess. Some Biblical names may include such names as Abraham, Joseph, Mary, and Sarah.

1. Before you become a parent, it's important to have or acquire excellent parenting skills. I would like to correct a common misconception that education begins at school. Education begins at home with parents. As a parent, you are your child's first teacher, so how and what you teach your child is important. An example of what and how to teach your child would be teaching your child his name, his mother's and father's name is of great importance. Also Parents should teach their children good manners which means respect for their teacher, class mates and themselves. It's important for your child to know about following rules. If parents teach their children basic rules, such as good manners and respect for their teacher and their classmates, then children will continue to build on these basic skills when they enter school.

Helpful Hints for Expectant Parents

1. Desire to be an awesome parent.
2. Be able to afford a child.
3. Have the proper prenatal care and proper insurance coverage for the birth of the child.
4. Get familiar with excellent parenting skills. This can be done by reading parenting books, attending parenting classes, and visiting parenting websites.

5. Set goals and plan for the child's education.
6. Plan for your baby to be in a healthy environment.
7. Do *not* be in an abusive relationship or unhealthy relationship.
8. If you're the mother, pamper your body by eating the proper diet and getting the proper rest and exercise. Wait patiently for the birth of the baby.

One of the most significant things those who want to become parents can do is get in the position so that the child will be healthy and parented in a wonderful environment. Nothing is guaranteed in life, but goal setting, planning, and preparation are great therapy for the mind and body. Goal setting is also magnificent for the baby that you will bring into the world. Goal setting gives the parent a chance to plan for their future as well as their children.

There are exceptions of parenting that are brought on by extraordinary situations, such as incest, rape, and teenage pregnancy. Exceptions in this case mean disapproval or stipulation. These unorthodox situations have to each be dealt with separately and given the best of consideration. Situations that are unorthodox are situations that are unapproved or unconventional.

Chapter 3

Infant and Toddler Development

———————— 📖 ————————

Some moms get an early start and begin reading to their newborn babies; some expectant moms even read to their unborn babies. As the baby's senses are developing in the brain, and the baby begins to develop into a toddler, the baby's cognitive growth is strengthened. The baby's brain becomes sensitive to the sounds that are pronounced by the parent. A baby recognizes his or her name and begins to recognize other words.

Language Development During an Infant's First Two Years

Birth to twenty-four months: When infants are born, crying is about the only language they have; infants and parents both depend on it. Crying tells the parents if something is wrong with their infant.

Two months: At two months infants still depend upon crying. Their crying becomes more intense. Infants also begin to smile at their parents as part of their language. Infants seem to understand their parents' sounds and words.

Three to four months: Babies begin to show signs of understanding by crying, hollering and making sounds that let the parents know their baby understands language.

Four to six months: Babies will say their first words. Some babies will say *da-da* as their first words; others will say *ma-ma*. Other babies will say other two-letter words. Some authors will call these two letter words babbling instead of words.

Six to twelve months: Babies begin to say longer words. Babies love when their parents or caregiver reads to them. Babies smile or laugh at their favorite nursery rhyme or favorite story. They start identifying characters in the stories their parents or caregiver reads. At this age they love to play with toys that make sounds and will notice the different sounds coming from toys. When taught by adults, babies will clap their hands and sing along with nursery rhymes and songs they like.

Twelve to eighteen months: Some toddlers are walking at twelve months, though some walk earlier and some later. As soon as the toddler learns to walk, he starts to run. Toddlers can now understand their parents or caregivers, when the adults play age-appropriate games with them.

Eighteen to twenty-four months: Toddlers are well on their way with learning language skills. They talk using more words and have begun to talk in sentences. Toddlers also show expressions by hitting, running, playing with large playground equipment, such as the merry-go-round and riding tricycles. These toddlers are enjoying their lives and having fun expressing this.

Toddlers learn language skills from adults. As parents or caregivers, it's important to use the correct language when talking and playing with your toddler. As you teach your toddler language skills, explain every detail in what you are teaching, such as size, color and shape. Your toddler, near or at the age of two, will be very inquisitive.

Toddlers in learning position with teacher.

As a parent, you should learn to recognize the signs of language development during your child's first two years so that you can watch for and mark off each step your infant and toddler takes. If some or even a few steps are not taken at or around the general time frame, it would be a good idea to visit your child's pediatrician for advice on what to do next. The doctor may recommend a speech and language therapist or that you should spend more time modeling the correct language sounds.

Early language intervention is an essential part of growth and development. If your infant's or toddler's needs are not met properly, your child's language skills might be affected into adulthood. Please don't let this happen to you and your child. An example of this would be, a child that has a speech problem of stuttering and stammering and does not have this speech problem corrected.

To avoid making mistakes in your child's development, read good parenting books and surf the internet for information on child development, including cognitive, physical, emotional, and social. Don't forget to confide in your child's pediatrician about any medical problem that your child may have. Your pediatrician can refer you to other child specialists if needed.

Schedule and keep all appointments with your toddler's pediatrician. This is very important because the pediatrician will check your child and remind you of the developmental stages to expect with your child. If your toddler is not developing his language skills properly, your pediatrician will recommend that you take your child to see a specialist. Following these basic rules of child development, should help complete your language goals for your child.

Toddler visiting his pediatrician.

Chapter 4

Educational Foundations

One of the most important attributes of education is a strong foundation. A foundation in education means a beginning, base, or start. Another excellent definition for foundation in education is the basics—language, reading, writing, and mathematics. My favorite two definitions are *beginning* and *base*, which would mean basics. You might ask, "Why is a great foundation so important?" Some educators might say, "When you don't get the basics at the beginning, you can make up for it in between or at the end of your high school education." Let me give you an example of this belief of making up in between or at the end of educational learning. If you are building a building and you skip the bottom or base, what kind of building would you have? Could you start building your building in between the bottom and middle, or could you start building at the end of your building? Would your building stand or crumble under pressure? Of course you can't build a building by skipping the base, and neither could you start in between the bottom and middle. Yes, your building would crumble under pressure if you were able to get it up.

An example of the crumbling process in education is a student failing a standardized test because he or she has insufficient basic skills. A solid foundation at the beginning of your child's education is of great importance.

Students are reading in the presence of the teacher.

Chapter 5

Different Types of Day Care

Day care is an institution that provides supervision and care of infants and young children during the day, particularly so that parents can hold jobs. The terms day care or childcare center and nursery school are often used interchangeably to identify various types of day care for children and for preschool educational programs.

Nursery school is a school for children, usually from birth to five and six years old.

Prekindergarten is a school that teaches the necessary cognitive social and physical skills usually from three to five years old in order to get kids ready for kindergarten.

Preschool is a school that teaches social, cognitive, and physical skills.

Preschool or prekindergarten are in some public schools.

They can also be found in nursery and day care schools or centers. Pre-k and prekindergarten have the same meaning.

Types of Day Care

Center-based care may be labeled as childcare, day care, nursery school, or preschool. These centers care for children in groups and usually have sponsors, such as universities, social service agencies, independent owners, and owners of large corporations. Some parents prefer center-based care because they believe that children are safer because of state regulations and inspections.

There should be no more than four infants per caregiver and no more than eight infants per one group of children in center-based care.

There should be no more than four young toddlers (ages twelve to twenty-four months) per caregiver, with a maximum of twelve young toddlers and three caregivers per group. The state recommends there be no more than six older toddlers and two caregivers per group. As the years pass by, state, local restrictions and regulations change to keep up with modern times. Also, states rules and regulations regarding childcare may differ in each state. However, basic rules are usually the same or similar.

Some of the adantages of center-base care are as follows:

1. The staff are trained and supervised.
2. More resources and equipment are available.
3. Care is still available when a staff member is absent.
4. The centers are more likely to be licensed and subject to state regulations.
5. Children in center-based care demonstrate slightly better cognitive development than those cared for in the home, possibly because they have more opportunity to interact with other children and are exposed to more learning materials.

Some of the disadvantages of center-based care are as follows:

1. The costs are higher than for other types of care.
2. The backgrounds of the staff can vary greatly, and there is often a greater turnover.
3. Larger groups of children may mean less individual attention for a child.
4. There is greater likelihood of exposure to communicable illnesses.

Family Childcare Providers

Family childcare providers offer care for children in the provider's home. Requirements differ from state to state, but the majority of states require that providers be regulated if they are watching more than four children. Over crowding in child care facilities can become a problem. "I think this is a good state law, and I also think that all states should have this state law in place. I think this will prevent tragedies from happening so often. You may have heard of the many tragedies that have happened lately concerning childcare providers. Families can be devastated from tragedies pertaining to the loss of their children. This is not just a family problem with children, but a problem for all tax-paying citizens as well as non-tax–paying citizens. It is the duty of the citizens of this country to help keep America safe. As a result of this, we as citizens can feel proud to be Americans. Problems in daycare, schools, both private and public affect all citizens as well as the school community. An example of this would be, "a school shooting at a neighborhood school." This violent attack would affect all students and administrators as well as all staff and other employees connected to the school. This attack would also affect the citizens in the school community as well as businesses in the community. This attack would affect all schools in the district as well as all citizens in the district.

As parents, our job should be to keep our children as safe as possible. Accidents have been known to happen when there are too many children cared for by family providers. Many states have a voluntary regulation process in place for those providers caring for four or fewer children. Regulations usually require providers to meet minimum health, safety, and nutrition standards. In addition, they are usually required to have a criminal background check. Some states yearly inspect the homes of family childcare providers, and many require on going training. Parents often make the choice of family care providers because of the more homelike environment offered. This childcare arrangement may be less expensive and offers a more flexible schedule. Some parents may also believe that their children are safer and more secure with a single provider in smaller groups.

The American Academy of Pediatrics recommends that family childcare providers should have six children or fewer per one adult caregiver, including the caregiver's own children. A childcare provider's total number of children should be less if infants and toddlers are involved. A childcare provider should care for no more than two children younger than two years of age.

State regulations differ from state to state. Make sure you check the regulations and stipulations that your state has in place for the type of childcare service that you choose. Nothing can take the place of an educated parent when it comes to choosing an effective and efficient childcare provider for your children. Your decision should coincide with your goals for your child in education as well as building your child's foundation for getting an incredible education.

Some of the advantages of family childcare are as follows:

1. There are usually fewer children in family childcare than center-based care.
2. There may be children of different ages.
3. The child gets to stay in a home environment.
4. Childcare may be less expensive, and a flexible schedule may be tolerated.

Some of the disadvantages of family childcare are as follows:

1. Many family childcare providers are not licensed or regulated.
2. Resources and equipment may not be available; Learning material such as books, and playground equipment, such as swings and slides are considered as resources and equipment.
3. Family childcare providers usually work alone, which make their work difficult to evaluate.
4. Regulations and stipulations that you want for your child's education may not be available.
5. Your child's educational goals may not be able to be met.

Relatives, Friends, and Neighbor Care

This type of care is provided by a relative, friend, or a neighbor and can take place in the child's home or the provider's home.

Some of the advantages of this kind of child care are:

1. Parents may believe their children are receiving more loving and affectionate care.
2. Parents may think a relative, friend, or neighbor may share the same values.
3. The child may receive one-on-one attention and care.
4. There may be a great deal of flexibility in this kind of childcare.

Some disadvantages of relatives, friends, and neighbor care are:

1. There are minimal regulations and stipulations required by most states.
2. There may be lack of care if the relative, friend, or neighbor gets sick or goes on vacation.
3. There may be a lack of childcare equipment or necessities for the child.
4. There may not be proper education taught for the child's age.

5. This type of childcare may have certain advantages but may not meet the standards for the goals and foundation-building that you have planned for your child.

Summary

There are different types of childcare, such as day care, nursery school and preschool. They all have advantages and disadvantages but they have one thing in common, which is to provide childcare for your children. You should be educated about the childcare business, if you plan to work, go to school, or otherwise be out of the home during the day. You will need to make one of the most important decisions in your child's life, so be a responsible and an educated parent.

Based on the goals you have made for yourself and your child, you will either choose to stay at home with your child and be the effective provider, or you will choose to be out of the home and provide your child with the most efficient childcare that you can afford. Remember, this period of your child's life is a critical part of the beginning of his education. Everything that your child learns or does not learn will affect his or her educational foundation. Your child's physical, cognitive, emotional, and social development are very important. It's crucial that parents choose a childcare facility after doing a thorough background check on the facility. Also, make sure that the childcare facility that you choose is aligned with the goals that you have set for your child in all development areas.

All childcare falls under day care. Day care is defined as a place for childcare, whether in an institution, a childcare center, or a school or in a provider's home, the child's home, or a relative's, neighbor's, or friend's home. Some daycare is monitored by the state, which is an advantage, whereas some daycare is not monitored by the state, such as daycare in some homes—in a relative's, friend's, or neighbor's home. Under the term day care are nursery schools and prekindergarten. In some nursery schools, regular education is provided through the sixth grade. Day care could also be in private schools or public schools. Day care refers to the care provided for infants, toddlers, preschoolers and school-aged children, and some after-school programs.

From my experience, one of the most important purposes of day care is providing the most efficient and effective care for working parents' children. Day care should mean that parents children are well cared for—the child's needs are met, such as being fed meals and snacks at the appropriate time. The child is kept clean and neat. The child's bathroom needs are met. The child's physical, emotional, and social needs are met. The child's language and mental skills, including cognitive skills, are met. The child learns as well as being cared for, and the child is happy and adjusting to being away from his or her parent. With this kind of daycare, your child is well on his or her way to building an effective foundation in education.

Chapter 6

Types of Development

When parents are educated in the area of early development of children, they can make the best decisions concerning the early education of their children.

Physical development has to do with the body's changing in proportions and appearance, functioning of body systems, perceptional motor capacities, and physical health.

Parents need to pay close attention to the stages of their children's physical growth. For an example, is your child crawling or walking within the age-appropriate time frame? Has your child made the adjustment to being potty trained at the appropriate age? Working parents will have more of a difficult time with this physical development because they are not able to spend enough time with their children to develop a pattern, unlike a stay-at-home parent who has the time to dedicate to this aspect of physical development.

Cognitive growth has to do with changes in intellectual abilities, including attention, memory, academics, everyday knowledge, problem solving, imagination, creativity, and language development. This stage of cognitive development plays a necessary part in the development stages. An example would be examining a toy for touching, feelings, and sounds. In this stage of development, the child is given a chance to explore, compete, think, and analyze. Some children can develop high-level thinking skills. If children are at a nursery or a basic day care, they probably won't be given chances that a child has at home with the parent.

Emotional and social development includes self-awareness, which is a central part of children's emotional and social growth. Children learn the aspects of their self and who they are in the environment. Being around other children in a day care will help them identify themselves as well as others. Self-awareness also provides the foundation for self-control. Self-control can be seen when children obey and comply with simple commands. Around eighteen months, the capacity for self-control appears, and it improves steadily into early childhood. In nursery and day care, children are taught to deal with their emotions through winning and losing in game playing. When children have proper training in early emotional and social growth, they are well on their way to building their foundation in early childhood development.

Now that I've explained the stages of a child's development, you can understand why it is often said that a parent is a child's first teacher. When a child is born, the first stage of cognitive development begins. If parents are knowledgeable about the early stages of child development, then they can be assured that their children are in the proper environment for the stages of child development to take place gracefully. An educated parent will know if their children are developing properly at the proper stage in their lives.

One can understand why a child entering preschool or kindergarten might have difficulty learning if their developmental stages have been neglected. Children who successfully go through their developmental stages will be ready to learn, grow, and continue to build their educational foundation.

In my teaching career I've seen that a child who masters maybe one or two stages of development will not be able to keep up with the grade level in which he or she has been placed. When this happens, the child has difficulty learning, and the child's teacher has a difficult time trying to teach this student.

I will emphasize that children's educational foundation is an urgent and necessary part of parents' goal setting for their children's future in education. If parents don't see the significance of this and understand early childhood development, and if they are not willing to become educated about it, then their children are at risk of being deprived of an awesome foundation in education. That is why federal, state, and local governments offer financial aid to some parents who cannot afford day care or nursery school and need to work. As a society in the twenty-first century, our main goal should be that all children get the best education possible.

Chapter 7

Development in Physical, Cognitive, and Emotional and Social Growth

Birth to six months: Physical development in infants and toddlers has to do with the body size, the functioning of the body and body systems. Physical growth is a way of keeping up with the overall of rapid growth that takes place.

During this period infants will begin to support their weight on their arms and lift their heads when placed on their stomachs. At six months, infants who are bottle fed will want to hold the bottle. At six months, infants begin to turn onto their stomachs. They also are scooting and getting ready to crawl. Infants love for parents to play with them. They also like for parents or day care providers to talk to them, read nursery rhymes and short stories to them, and act out the characters in the stories—this is exciting and entertaining to six-month-old infants.

Six to twelve months: Infants of this age will learn how to sit up straight and begin to crawl. Some infants will pull themselves up and stand. If there is a small table nearby, infants will stand and balance themselves by holding on to the table. In this period, some infant will begin to walk. In this period of time, infants are growing rapidly.

Thirteen to eighteen months: Infants become toddlers at this age. Toddlers should be walking at eighteen months and be able to identify their body parts. If toddlers are not walking at eighteen months, parents should take their toddler to see the pediatrician. Parents should make sure their toddlers wear the correct shoes such as shoes that support the infant's arch if needed. Toddlers should be encouraged to walk. Some toddlers will need to hold their parents' hand or a caregiver's hand as they walk. Learning to walk is a major stage of child development. Therefore, toddlers should be helped and watched closely while going through this stage of development.

Nineteen to twenty-four months: Toddlers' motor skills will be fairly developed. Some toddlers will begin to use the bathroom at this time, but some will take longer before they're toilet trained. If your toddler is not using the bathroom within this time frame, don't become discouraged; just continue to have patience and work with your toddler. All toddlers are not the same. Toddlers' motor skills develop at different rates, some slower and others faster. Some toddlers may be three, four, five, or even six years old before they use the bathroom exceptionally well. Toddlers will learn how to play games of running, just to see how fast that they can run.

Birth to six months: Cognitive development at this stage is basic actions such as sucking, grasping, looking and listening. The infants will let the parents know by crying if their needs are not met. Infants get used to the sounds and language of their environment. Using correct and fluent language around infants is very important. An infant's form of communication is through crying if something is wrong or a pleasant expression if everything is fine.

Seven to twelve months: Cognitive development for toddlers at this age are still going through basic actions such as listening and trying to grasp whatever knowledge that they can that will help them to continue to make progress on the skills that they have learned. Toddlers try to walk or already are walking. Some toddlers at this age are in day care and some are at home with a parent. In day care, toddlers begin to play with other toddlers. At home, toddlers begin to play with their parents, or they will play alone. They begin to follow directions. At day care, toddlers learn how to sit in circles and listen to nursery rhymes and stories. They participate by playing the characters in the stories. Toddlers at this age level learn colors and shapes, and they also learn how to count using numbers. They listen to the sounds of words and pronounce words. They put words together to make sentences. All of these ways of child development coincide with natural responses of children in their environment. Natural development coincides with cognitive development. As time passes, children learn, grow and develop. At this stage of development, toddlers learn rapidly.

Thirteen to eighteen months: Cognitive development—toddlers at this age are usually walking and are able to play with toys. Toddlers now enjoy assembling blocks and building things. They continue to learn counting and their ABC's. Toddlers continue to develop their vocabulary. They talk in more complete sentences. Toddlers at this stage also learn rapidly.

Cognitive development; Cognitive development begins in an infant through basic reflexes, senses, and motor responses. As the infant and toddler grow and interact with the environment, rapid growth occurs and continues through childhood. The child continues to learn and discover new things daily through cognitive development.

Nineteen to twenty-four months: Cognitive development in this stage of dramatic growth and learning is continued. Kids in this cognitive stage love to play with toys, work puzzles, and draw. They love to play games on their parents' phones. Toddlers are building things out of blocks and enhancing their art skills of drawing. Toddlers learn about having friends and learn about having a good friend. Having a good friend seems to be very important to them. Toddlers learn how to be creative and how to solve problems. Toddlers at this age are inquisitive about everything. They show the emotions of shame and embarrassment. Toddlers at this age are very friendly and have to be watched closely.

Birth to six months, Emotional and social development from birth to six months is the bond that the infant shares with the parent or the caregiver. Infants at this stage show signs of emotions, such as happiness sadness and anger. Usually when an infant is happy, he smiles, and when an infant is sad, or angry, he cries or hollers out. Infants love attention and they love to be talked to and caressed. If there are siblings in the home, infants love to play with them. They are bonding with their siblings. Infants are definitely learning how to socialize.

Seven to twelve Months, Emotional and social development in infants continue to develop. Infants at this stage show more emotions than previously to get what they want. For instance if they want to play ball. If they see a ball, they will begin playing with it. Infants are learning to sit at the table in a high chair and eat. Infants love to play games with parents or caregivers, such as patty-cake. Infants are learning. new words and building their vocabulary up. Infants are experiencing more emotions and becoming more sociable as they develop.

Thirteen to eighteen months: Emotional and social growth takes off at a faster level as infants develop into toddlers. Toddlers at this age begin to notice gender and they begin to pick their friends. Toddlers emotions are developing and they begin to pick group play such as playing kick ball with their friends. Toddlers enjoy playing games on their parents cell phones. Toddlers will stay busy from eight to ten hours a day. This is quite a few hours for an eighteen to twenty four months old toddler. Rapid growth at this period, socially and emotionally takes place.

Nineteen to twenty-four months: Emotional and social development of toddlers at this age, which is noted as the "terrible twos" is not a good title for toddlers at this stage of development. Toddlers are learning about friends and having a very good friend. They learn how to solve problems' and how to be creative. Toddlers like to feel good about themselves, so positive comments are very important to them. They are learning new sounds and words daily. Toddlers lives are very busy, exciting and interesting. They need all of the understanding they can get. They love their parents, and if they attend daycare, they love their teachers. Toddlers keep building on experiences that they already have.

Students are playing soccer ball with the coach

These stages of development for infants and toddlers are part of their educational foundation with which all parents should become familiar. These stages are a guide for parents as their children go from one stage to another. If your child is not developing according to these guidelines, it may be wise to get help from a professional in the field of child development. Early detection is a lifesaver in any life situation. It's certainly a basic rule that applies in the education of your child. Most of the time, parents detect 95 percent of abnormalities in their children before school age, and if they do, professional help is recommended. If a parent does not have insurance or good health care, there are organizations that will help. Each state will usually have insurances for children at a discount that parents can get that need it. The children's Health Insurance Program [CHIP] is a partnership between the federal and state governments that provides low cost health coverage to children in families. Also that provides low cost health coverage to children in families that earn too much money to qualify for medicaid.

Remember, parents are their children's provider as well as their first teachers. As a parent, thinking that someone else will do your job would not be a correct assumption. Some of these issues are simple things such as seeing your child's pediatrician for check-ups and keeping up with your child's shot record. Parents should also notice differences in their child's vision or they could notice differences in their child's speech. There are some great and fantastic teachers, but why depend on them to do what you can do for your child? Even if a teacher recognizes your child's disability or development problem, will it be early enough to correct the problem? Your child has a better chance of getting a superb education if you are attentive and educate yourself in early childhood development.

If all parents follow these guidelines, they can expect their children to excel in school and to master all stages of childhood development at the correct time.

Chapter 8

Terrible Twos and Your Toddler

Everything that you have heard about the terrible twos probably has been negative because there hasn't been enough positive information provided. We may ask the age of a child, and when we hear the age two, we immediately think of the terrible twos.

Two is an age that we have all been through, and our children will have to do the same. Do you realize that being two is part of the early development of a child? Have you done research on which developmental stage your two-year-old is in? If you do this, then some of the negative talk will become positive talk.

No parent looks forward to the terrible twos, which begins sometime in the toddler years. Parents don't expect this stage until after the toddler turns two, but the terrible twos could begin at any time during the child's second year or before.

This is where parent education and knowing what to look for becomes helpful.

Toddlers at this stage are known to be defiant, rebellious, and stubborn. They don't exhibit this behavior intentionally but because of the developmental stage they are in. Their language skills are limited, so they are not able to express their emotions as do older children. Two year old children's emotions are not yet developed. They may become frustrated easily and may resort to biting, hitting, kicking, and screaming. This type of behavior is called a temper tantrum, and it appears when toddlers don't get what they want. Most of the time when toddlers turn three or four years old, they will have matured and passed through the terrible-twos stage.

Learning more about this normal stage of development could make it easier for you and your child. The following are some tips that will help your toddler during this stage:

Use a schedule so that your toddler does things at or around the same time each day; for instance, nap, play, exercise, lunch, and learning time. This gives toddlers a sense of control and balance. They soon will remind their parents or providers of the scheduled routine. Also, let toddlers choose the type of snacks they would like and do the kind of exercise that they like. This helps toddlers make decisions and enjoy their power.

Do's and Do not's for Your Toddler

Do teach your toddler how to follow rules at home and at day care.

Don't give in to temper tantrums. Let your toddler know that rules still stand.

Do use time out and take away privileges, if needed.

Do show your toddler love and affection.

Do provide your toddler with a safe environment.

Don't leave your child unattended.

Physical Activities for Toddlers in the Terrible Twos

There are many great physical activities for toddlers in the terrible twos development stage. Some indoor activities include reading, counting, singing, drawing, coloring, finger painting, and dancing. Some outdoor activities include running, skipping, playing tag, and playing hide-and-seek. These activities can be played with a group or individually. Please take note that some children will leave a group and proceed to play alone.

Toddlers need to learn the difference between structured play and unstructured play. Structured play includes activities such as reading, counting, finger painting, drawing, and coloring. The toddler's environment is quiet, making it easy to concentrate with structured play. Unstructured play activities are skipping, running, jumping, leaping, and playing tag and hide-and-seek. Toddlers love these unstructured activities because they can play as they please and get satisfaction while playing these activities. Learning the difference between structured and unstructured activities will help kids recognize which activities require quietness, and which activities do not. On the basis of this analysis, kids will enjoy all activities and will realize the joy of quietness and noisiness. They will be happier and less bored. If toddlers are kept busy and guided into structured and unstructured activities, they will have less time to suffer frustration and temper tantrums. Introduce activities to your toddler and give him the opportunity to choose which activity he wants to engage in. Remember, since your two-year-old is not able to express his emotions yet, you will need patience and understanding as you guide your toddler through the terrible twos.

Toddlers are involved in a learning experience with the teacher.

Toddlers are playing together supervised by the teacher.

Chapter 9

Attention Deficit/Hyperactivity Disorder (ADHD)

Attention deficit/hyperactivity disorder, often referred to as ADHD, is puzzling to parents, teachers, and doctors, and it's hard to diagnose. ADHD is a developmental disorder that may be found in children before the age of seven. If children have little or no intervention, then ADHD may continue into adulthood.

There are different types of this disorder:

- ADHD—the most common type, which combines all the symptoms
- Inattentive ADHD, which is recognized by impaired attention and concentration
- Hyperactive-impulsive ADHD, without inattentive

Clynie Huggins

ADHD is one of the most commonly studied developmental disorders in toddlers and school-age children. It affects 3–5 percent of children globally. ADHD is a serious disorder of behavior. If you suspect your child is suffering from this disorder, seek professional help immediately. The professional will help to distinguish normal behavior from abnormal behavior. Remember, the sooner you seek a professional, the sooner your child can receive help.

ADHD treatment usually consists of some combination of medications, behavior modification, and counseling with a professional. Not all professionals are in favor of prescribing medication for this condition. This decision will be left up to the parent and the professional, whether it is a medical doctor or a psychologist.

As a teacher, I have experienced many cases of ADHD in children. This disorder can be disruptive as well as harmful to individuals in this environment. Some ADHD students may act out this disorder if they are angered. This anger could cause them to speak out out, or even start a fight. If your child is in a public school, this is usually the procedure that would take place. The teacher and another professional (a nurse, a counselor, or both) should arrange a conference with the parent of the child. In the conference, the teacher would let the parent know the symptoms of the student. This would include a written record of the symptoms in detail for six weeks and the date and time of each symptom or incident. An intervention plan would be put into motion for the child. The plan would include numerous suggestions that could help the child with his or her behavior problems. A date would be made for another conference to see if the intervention plan helped. If the first intervention plan did not work, then an appointment should be scheduled for the child with a professional child psychologist.

Chapter 10

Autism

Autism or *autism spectrum disorder* (ASD) is a pervasive developmental disorder that also is classified in a group of complex disorders of the brain. ASD is usually found in children between two and three years of age. This disorder is under research to better understand it, even before it emerges in children. Autism awareness is a key research item, in which clinical doctors, parents, and volunteers are helping with the outcome of this research.

Asperger syndrome, or ASD is also associated with intellectual disability such as difficulties in motor coordination, attention and physical health issues, such as sleep and gastrointestinal disturbances.

There is a growing increase of children with ASD, according to US statistics. There is no explanation given for this increase. Also more boys suffer with ASD as well as ADHD. There is no explanation for this outcome.

Research now claims that a number of rare gene changes are associated with ASD.

Some risk factors associated with autism are the ages of both parents when the baby is conceived, illnesses during pregnancy, a difficult pregnancy, and if the mother has an unhealthy immune system.

Children with autism may have verbal disability and may not be able to take care of themselves as do other children of the same age. There tends to be a variety of anxiety disorders in children. Also, specific phobia is a common condition associated with ASD. Mood disorders associated with depression may be seen in lower-level and high-level ASD. The child may exhibit behavior problems such as not following orders and showing stubbornness.

ASD and ADHD are two of the most common developmental disorders in children between the ages of two to six. Parents need to be educated in this area, as parents are the child's first teacher. If you, the parent think that your child's behavior is not developing as it should, then your next step should be to get professional help. Educating yourself in child development will help you to understand normal behavior. If your child attends public school, the teacher can help you with keeping a record of symptoms and incidents. When you take your child to see a professional, your child will be diagnosed and a proper management plan will be put into action to help your child. With effective learning tactics, your child can then proceed to develop in the proper way.

If your child is in public school, after the recommendation of the child's teacher, an ARD meeting will be called. ARD stands for Admission, Review and Dismissal process for children. This ARD meeting will consist of the parent, teacher, and one other professional, who will come up with a plan that will be beneficial to the student and all involved. The ARD committee can recommend that the student be tested, with the parent's approval, by a professional. After the results are in, then a decision will be made again in another ARD meeting of the outcome, and proper placement of the student will take place. This is the process that takes place in having a student tested for Special Education in public schools. Most behavioral disorders in children such as ASD and ADHD are classified as Special Education, so if a student is in public school, the testing, diagnostics and review plus, placement will be done by the Special Education Department. The other group members will need to agree upon the diagnostics of the professional at this time.

Students are participating in a science project.

Chapter 11

Rules for Children

Setting rules for your household as soon as your child is able to understand, even before your child can talk, is a great idea.

At two months, infants make cooing and babbling sounds. Parents talk back to the infants and even use some sign language. Parents start to make rules of proper and improper behavior at this stage, making the infants understand. As the infant child develops into a toddler, an educated parent will continue to make more strenuous rules of proper and improper conduct. Parents make rules when they start to teach their children childhood games, such as pat-a-cake and peek-a-boo.

Personality development takes place from infancy to two years of age, so it is imperative that the parent or caregiver give the infant the love and attention that he or she needs.

Nurturing and the teaching of rules, including setting boundaries, will cause the child to develop an excellent learning personality, which is of great significance. A child who develops a personality geared toward learning and who has been taught to obey rules at home or in childcare will have a smoother transition to public or private school.

The parent or childcare provider will need to teach the child that rules should be respected and obeyed at home, in childcare, and at school. If a child is having problems in this area, the parent or childcare provider should dedicate more time to helping the child to understand the importance of rules and the consequences of not obeying them. Rules can be difficult for some children to understand as well as obey. But parents need to recognize that some areas of child development are not easy. Some will just happen naturally, but other areas will be difficult and take time. Children need to understand that our society is made of rules and regulations that everyone follows, including adults.

In some schools, teachers are burdened trying to teach children how to develop good personalities and how to conduct themselves in the classroom, instead of teaching the curriculum for that grade level. If teachers have to teach children behavior skills that should already have been taught and learned, then there will be less time to teach children the learning material. This is why education in child development is critical, and parents should see that their children are taught properly in order to develop the skills they need for the future.

Teachers are hired to teach the educational curriculum, but in some schools, this is difficult to do because of students' social backgrounds. Some students refuse to follow class rules or school rules. Their attitudes and behavior are obnoxious and detrimental to learning. Some of these students do everything that they can to prevent the educational system from doing it's job. Not only do they hurt themselves or stop themselves from getting an education, but they stop other students from getting their education. This kind of behavior should be reported to the proper authorities and definitely something should be done about this.

Most parents and citizens are aware of the cases of bullying that have happened in this twenty-first century. This is not what parents and citizens want to hear or read about. We want to send our children to school to learn and to become active and model students who can help build a prominent future for themselves and this society. We also want our children to be safe as well as feel safe.

In my opinion, students who present themselves as bullies and act out with deadly conduct probably have an abnormality in mental health. It's crucial for parents to monitor their children's physical, cognitive, emotional, and social development of all ages. If you see an abnormality in your child's development process, talk with your pediatrician for advice. Again, parents, please read closely about abnormalities in behavior because all behavior abnormalities are not the same. Abnormalities in personality mean differences or unusual. An example of this behavior problem would be; a six or seven year old student crying and hollering all day or half of the day at school. If the behavior problem can be solved at home, then parents should take the time to solve the problem; If the behavior problem cannot be corrected, then an appointment with a specialist is needed.

All parents with children need to be educated in early childhood development. If there are abnormalities with your child, take the next step of early detection to fix the problem. This could mean small problems that you as a parent can fix, or it could mean making an appointment with a medical doctor, psychologist, or counselor or a conference with your child's teacher. Whatever type of intervention is needed, please don't waste precious time; just do what's necessary for your child.

Remember that learning begins at home and that a parent is a child's first teacher. Personality and behavior development also begin at home. It's crucial to give serious attention to this part of your child's development process.

High school students are participating
in a medical assignment.

Each school has its set of rules, as does each class. These rules need to be obeyed in order to make the school efficient and effective in educating students. Schools have to be accountable to the school district and to the state and federal governments. Public schools, as well as some charter schools, fall into this accountability system. Any school that's accepting help or funding from the state or federal government is held accountable by a set of rules. These rules include attendance and test scores.

Test scores are one of the most significant accountability instruments used to determine how well the student is doing, as compared to students in the same district and on the state and national level. Public schools within the district are allocated funds from the state and federal governments, based on the number of students enrolled. All schools funded by the state and federal government struggle to keep numbers of students high. Ethnic groups also play an important part in the distribution of funds.

Parents and students need to understand why rules are made and why they are expected to follow them. Rules govern our society. They are responsible for moving our society in the way that it should go. If rules are not followed, then there are consequences that we will have to be accountable for. All class and school rules should be obeyed. A copy of school rules should be placed in the main front office of each school on a bulletin board, and a copy of class rules should be placed on a bulletin board in each classroom. It is very important that a copy of school and class rules be sent home at the beginning of each school year. These school and class rules should be read and discussed with each student and his or her parents. These rules should serve as a guide for your child's school and classes. These school and class rules will make parents knowledgeable of what the expectations are for their children at school.

Parents should remind their children of the importance of these rules. Parents can also discuss the consequences for not obeying these rules. As parents, your children need to know that you are interested in their education in every aspect. I believe that when children know their parents are involved with daily activities in school, they will develop a positive attitude toward school and will try harder to do well. In my experience as a teacher, I've seen that most children want to make their parents and grandparents proud of them. As parents, it's especially important to take an active part in your child's daily education.

Chapter 12

Choice of Schools

Parents have to choose from different types of schools for their children. There are public schools and magnet schools, which are usually within the districts of the public schools. These include schools that focus on law enforcement, medical, math, science, technology, agriculture, health, and music. There are many more schools like these for your children if you prefer these types of schools. There also are alternative schools. These schools usually have students that can not adjust to the regular school students, and these schools may have smaller classes. There are schools that specialize in sports training for students who will play professional sports. Parents need to take time and find the best school that will help their children reach their potential in the area for which parents and their children have set educational goals for.

As a parent, if you have picked out a school for your child

Clynie Huggins

for advancement in their educational future, and that school does not meet your standards, then change schools. After all, this is your child's future, and it must be monitored. Changes must be made in the best interest of your child. There are vanguard schools in some school districts. These schools are for gifted and talented students.

Also, there is a special education school or program. Special education is usually funded by the federal government. This school can be a separate school or a school program within a school. This school is for children who have serious or mild learning disabilities, such as in reading and math, or speech disabilities. Also, students with behavioral disorders are under Special Education. There are some severely physically and mentally handicapped students, as well as less severe students in special education. Some of the more severe cases for the physically handicapped students require special equipment and more teachers or teacher aides to help care for these students. The same thing is true for the mentally challenged students. Some special education departments have started mainstreaming students who have mild learning disabilities into the regular classroom. This means the special education student's program is modified so that he or she is able to keep up with regular education students, with the help of the teacher. Mainstreaming students with mild disabilities into the regular class room is an advantage for those students. This means that with special modification, these students are able to learn beside the regular education students and be successful in learning.

Students with serious learning disabilities, such as functioning two or three grade levels behind the regular education students, will have a difficult time keeping up in a mainstreaming program. These students would need special help or participation in a special program to bring them up to grade level. The seriousness of the disability determines the type of program for which the student would qualify.

Parents with students who qualify for special education will need to take an active part in their child's education. The parent will need to attend all ARD meetings for their child and take an active part in the meetings. An appropriate decision and educational plan designed by the ARD committee will be put into action, along with testing to determine the area of the child's disabilities.

Public schools get their funding from local taxes, state and federal government funding. Ninety percent of children today attend public school. Children attend a particular school according to the boundary lines set by the school district. In later years, students may attend other schools in the same district if there is space for the student and certain qualifications are met. Parents are required to furnish transportation.

Charter schools have become popular in the last fifteen years in the United States. These schools are publicly funded and must meet certain performance standards set by the state. Unlike the public school system, charter schools are free from the traditional standards set for public schools.

Some students are home schooled, and the parents are usually their children's teachers.

Online learning allows students to learn on the computer instead of a regular classroom.

Magnet schools are well noted for their special programs. These are public schools that are highly selective and very effective for teaching skilled subjects in particular areas that are not offered in regular schools such as mathematics, art, and science. Magnet schools began in the early 1970s to help integrate public schools by encouraging students to attend schools other than the neighborhood schools. In later years, some neighborhood schools became magnet schools to keep neighborhood schools in existence.

Private schools rely on tuition payments and funds from nonpublic sources, such as grants, endowments, and charitable donations. Private schools select their students.

Independent schools are private schools governed by nonprofit boards of trustees.

Parochial schools are church-related schools. The most common type is owned and operated by Catholic parishes or dioceses, but some are operated by Protestant denominations. Students attending Catholic schools do not have to be Catholic, but they will be required to attend religious education classes and prayer services.

Proprietary schools are private schools that are run for profit. They do not have board members or trustees to answer to.

Chapter 13

Public Schools vs. Private Schools

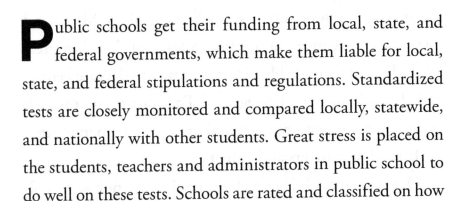

Public schools get their funding from local, state, and federal governments, which make them liable for local, state, and federal stipulations and regulations. Standardized tests are closely monitored and compared locally, statewide, and nationally with other students. Great stress is placed on the students, teachers and administrators in public school to do well on these tests. Schools are rated and classified on how well each school does.

In recent years, public schools have been given stipends for their students who do well on these tests. These stipends are usually divided among the teachers and administrators at these schools.

Attendance is another important stipulation required in funding for public schools. Attendance is monitored closely at public schools and Federal grants are awarded to some schools based on student attendance.

Statistics about each school and the district itself can be found on line. Free lunch and breakfast are provided at public schools, depending upon parent income. Income is not a factor of a student being excepted at a public school. Special programs, special education, neighborhood and volunteer participation, and parent/teacher organizations are also available in public schools. Participation in the Boy Scouts and Girl Scouts is affiliated with public schools. Some public high schools concentrate on having the best sports teams, such as football, basketball, baseball, softball, and soccer. This means scouting for professional ball is a great possibility. At some public schools, there are daycare centers and after-school tutorial programs. There are programs such as music, instrument training, and many more programs that are helpful to students and parents.

One other very influential mechanism for public schools is the regularly scheduled board meetings that parents may attend. This is great for parents who want to know the district's business. In some districts' at school board meetings, after the district has finished its business, parents or others in attendance may voice any concerns they may have.

Most public schools hire excellent teachers. Of course, experience is a valuable tool for teachers. The more years, teachers teach, the more years of experience they have. They are expected to do a better job than a first-year teacher or an inexperienced teacher. Until about fifteen or twenty years ago, experienced teachers were well respected and were praised for their dedication and longevity in education, but that has changed for most experienced teachers and administrators. They now seem to be less respected and less needed, and this has caused some teachers to retire early and permanently.

Why not keep experienced teachers so that test scores could continue to climb and then gradually bring in inexperienced teachers who can be trained by experienced teachers. This way, administrators, teachers, students, parents, and everyone involved would gain and grow in dignity, as would the school community. This would also take away stress from all teachers and administrators, experienced or inexperienced. Can you imagine how happy and overjoyed the students, administrators, teachers and parents would be?

Public schools are super schools, and they play a magnificent role in this society, providing free education for everyone and providing the type of education that each individual child needs, regardless of background, ethnicity, or financial status. The public school system tries to make sure that all students get the best education possible. The public school system does not offer just one type of school but a variety. Parents can choose the best type of school that will benefit their child the most in their career and their education. Parents can look forward to public schools' help in aligning their children with the educational goals set in elementary on through high school. This order of success should lead children to higher education, such as college, university, junior college, or trade school education.

Private schools receive their funds from tuition payments and funds from private donors and nonpublic sources, such as religious organizations, grants, endowments, and charitable donations. Private schools include parochial schools. According to the National Center for education ten percent of of U.S. students attend private school and ninety percent of students attend Public schools. This assessment was taken in 2013 and was updated in 2017. The U. S. Department of Education projects that in 2021, private schools will enroll about nine percent of pre-k- through twelfth grade and public school will enroll ninety one percent. Independent schools are also private schools. Usually when parents consider private schools, they look at the reputation and college preparation. Other things include class size, safety, special programs, location, and ideology. In choosing a private school, parents also decide on whether or not they want their children to have religious and or moral instruction. The most common type of religious school is run by the Catholic Church. Some private schools are known as boarding schools because they offer lodging. Private schools that focus on academic preparation are called prep schools.

Private schools try not to admit disturbed, unruly children

who might monopolize teachers' attention. Very few unruly students slip through, and those that do are expelled as soon as they begin to disrupt school routine or the lives of other children.

In private schools, academic achievement is the primary goal. There are very few sports, but some private schools have started participating in more activities. Students dedicate most of their time to academics. Every student tries to achieve and get the attention of the teacher and his or her parents.

Private schools require all children to take a core curriculum of English, mathematics, history, science, foreign language, music, and art from kindergarten through high school. Electives at the high school level are limited to additional courses in those disciplines. Children are not given any choice away from the educational building blocks that they already have.

Private schools are not governed by standardized tests, as public schools are.

Private-school students are average students, unlike the social and economic factors that society portrays them as having. Parents of private school students are not necessarily wealthy but are presumed to make a comfortable living. The parents of private school students who *are* wealthy think that their children can get a better education at a private school. It's up to the parents to choose the best school—wherever they think their children will get the best education possible.

Chapter 14

A Guide for Parents in Determining a Good School

A good school has the following:

- Strong and professional administrators and teachers
- A strong and diverse curriculum that will promote excellent participation and involvement from parents and community groups
- An excellent assessment system that shows growth and good scores when compared locally and on the state and national levels
- A balanced budget that is sufficient for the entire year
- A productive and conductive school climate that promotes learning

A good school has strong professional administrators.

Some schools are managed by one administrator—the principal—or sometimes by more than one principal or administrator. For example, most elementary schools have one principal, while middle schools and high schools usually have several principals and administrators.

1. The principal's job is to facilitate the school through the design and implementation of the curriculum and see that the resources needed are available. Also, the principal ensures that the teachers needed to teach the curriculum are hired.

2. The principal is responsible for professional and staff development needed to implement the curriculum in all components concerning the school.

3. The principal is responsible for producing correct documents for each business transaction done at the school.

4. In most cases, the principal is responsible for hiring all teachers, other administrators, staff, and other help for the operation of the school.

5. The principal is responsible for school participation in all district programs and seeing that the programs are monitored properly to ensure proper scope and sequence.

6. The principal is responsible for implementing all extracurricular school programs.

7. The principal is responsible for implementation of the correct assessments and correct scoring and recording of documentation.

8. The principal is responsible for gathering and recording correct demographic data.

9. The principal is responsible for the proper implementation of all technology, telecommunications, and information systems to facilitate the campus curriculum.

10. The principal is responsible for all class scheduling of the school's programs.

11. The principal is responsible for leading and guiding the school according to his or her vision in all components of school design.

12. The principal is responsible for setting the culture of the school and nurturing the culture according to his or her vision.

13. The principal is responsible for the motivation of innovative ideas and supporting higher-level thinking skills.

14. The principal is responsible for the faculty, staff, and school community acknowledgment and celebration of the contributions of students.

15. The principal is responsible for ensuring that parents and members of the community are active in the articulation of setting a vision to create and promote excellent learning.

16. The principal is responsible for using student assessment for formative and summary evaluation.

17. The principal is responsible for creating and managing the school campus's budget.

18. The principal is responsible for the safety of all students, faculty, and staff.

19. The principal is responsible for the daily operation of the school, including the plant operation and the cafeteria operation.

20. The principal is responsible for the facilitation of promoting decision making on analytical data. (Bosman, Robert, and Charles R. Berryman, "THE PERCIEVED CONCERNS OF ELEMENTARY SCHOOL PRINCIPALS AND ELEMENTARY SCHOOL TEACHERS TOWARD MAINSTREAMINING 1979.ED. 193 795")

These are just some of the important duties of the principal. There are many more. A principal's job is never completed.

Professional teachers are expected to meet the following requirements:

1. Teachers should have the correct credentials for teaching.
2. Recognize students who need extra or special help.
3. Recognize the importance of teaching the curriculum.
4. Know the importance of having supplementary material.
5. Provide students with ample learning materials.
6. Help students complete classwork.
7. Give homework as an extended activity.
8. Post the objectives of the lessons being taught.
9. Allow students the opportunity to practice the lessons.
10. Use different types of teaching methods when necessary.
11. Give students the proper tests and assessments.
12. Post class and school schedules on bulletin board.
13. Keep a substitute teacher's folder with current lessons.
14. Check and grade student's classwork and homework.
15. Make appointments with parents about students' progress.
16. Keep documentation of students' behavior.
17. Maintain good discipline in and out of the classroom.
18. Keep an atmosphere for learning and developing.
19. Use testing and assessments as an evaluation tool.
20. Ensure a school climate that's conducive to learning.
21. Introduce and create problem solving.
22. Treat all students equally, regardless of race or religion.

23. Incorporate technology to help enhance daily class.

24. Help students to work on their career interests.

25. Attend staff and professional development.

26. Continue higher education to strengthen teaching skills (These professional skills were written by the author, Clynie Huggins.)

Professional teachers should have many more good teaching skills. These are some of great significance.

These students are very happy graduating from high school.

Chapter 15

School Safety Rules

I.   Before enrolling your child in a new school, always check the data on line, the statistics and status of the school.

II.   School, class and safety rules should be given to all students at the beginning of the school year.

III. Teachers may set up conferences on the telephone or on line if parents are not able to come in person to the school.

IV.   Parent groups, such as PTO's or PTA's should have organized meetings pertaining to the safety and success of the school that they are zoned too.

V.   A school plan for student violence should be discussed and should be put into place as an action plan.

VI.   All school students, and all school employees should practice fire drills and all other safety drills often.

VII.   No weapons of any type should be allowed on any campus of a school in a student's possession.

VIII. If weapons are found of any type on a campus, the proper school authorities should be called or notified immediately.

IX.   If there is school violence on campus, the proper school authorities should be called or notified immediately.

X.   If there is violence on campus, the school safety plan should be put into action immediately.

XI.   All schools should be armed with safety devices such as door monitors and cameras, panic buttons and other safety devices.

XII. Bullying should not be allowed in schools and on school campuses.

XIII. Bullying should be reported to the proper school authorities.

XIV. Bullying cases should be handled by the proper authorities.

XV.   School districts, school administrators, teachers and staff, management departments, parent groups, and the business and school community should all work together for the safety and benefit of the students and everyone involved. ("School Safety Rules") written by the Author, Clynie Huggins

Chapter 16

Summary

The beginning of the book is about the history of early education in the United States. This includes where educated started, and the government official that played an important part in getting education started. This government official was Thomas Jefferson. Thomas Jefferson was the third president of the United Stated from March 4th, 1801 through March 4th 1809.

The two most common types of childhood disabilities was identified and discussed in detail. This gives parent a head start in noticing any abnormalities that their child may have.

Parents education in child developments should make them aware of all stages of child development. Parents should evaluate their own child's situation and decide which stage of development their child is in, and start from there, with goals for your child. Make goals that will enhance your child's ability and career.

This can be done by reading excellent parenting books on line, from libraries and other good sources. Once you do this, you have taken the first steps in getting educated in child development. Examine the behavior stage that your child is in and then work with your child accordingly. This means taking control of your child's behavior to help your child have a smooth transition from one stage to the next stage. If you haven't set goals and made rules for your child, do so at this time.

Remember, it's time to make sure that your child receives the highest quality of education that's possible. Parents, do the best that you can to implement the goals that you have set for your child's education. Make the necessary goals that will enable your child to have an educational foundation that that will produce the kind of behavior at school that will be conducive to learning. Make sure the school that your child attends is the type of school that your child can succeed in. If you send your child to daycare make sure the daycare is in compliance with your educational goals for your child. By taking the necessary steps with your child, he or she should be on their way to getting the highest quality of education that the twenty first century is demanding.

Parents, help your child to recognize his or her abilities and talents. In doing so, you can do a thorough job of planning, such as choosing the type of school that will be effective in your child's educational career. Also, looking forward to your child's career in higher education will be proof of the necessary goals and plans made in the beginning and on through your child's elementary and secondary education.

References

"Autism Spectrum," date accessed, 2/20/2012, p. 1-16, Autism Spectrum- Wikipedia, the free encyclopedia, URL, http://en.wikipedia.org/wiki/Autism-Spectrum

"Attention Deficit," American Psychiatric Association, (2013) Diagnostic and Statistical Manual of Mental Disorder (5th. ed.) Arlington : American Psychiatric Publishing p. 59-65. IS BN 978-0-89042-555-8, date accessed, 05/20/ 2014

"Public School" Versus "Private School," https:/blog/public-school-private-school, updated, 11/01/2018 by Grace Chen, 06/16/2019

"Day Care – baby, Definition, Description, Types of day-care, Encyclopedia of Children's Health," URL, http://www.healthofchildren.com/D/Day-Care.html P.1-6 date accessed, 2/2/2012

"Gale's Encyclopedia of Children's Health" https// www. cengage.com/...Product Overview.do www.healthofchildren. com/, accessed 12/13/2018

"Indicators of Child, Family, and Community connections Family, Work, and Child Care:

"United States Department of Health and Human Services, 2004. Available online at http://aspehhs.gov/hsp/ccquality-indo2/(accessed January 11, 2012

"Terrible Two's and Your Toddler Ages and Stages "Pediatrics, About.com by Iannell, Vincent, M. D. updated March 13,2005. date accessed, 02/20/2012_ http: baby parenting. about.com/od/activitiesandplay/u/toddler-activities.htm, 2/14/2012,

Verywell family, "Toddlers and the Terrible Twos, Consistency Can Help You Cope With Behavior Problems by Vincent Iannelli, MD Updated June 29, 2019, date accessed, July,10, 2019 WWW.VERYWELLFAMILY.COM accessed July11, 2019. dash Very Well is part of the Dotdash publishing Family

About.com. Toddlers and Twos Toddlers activities, https// babyparenting.about.com/od/activitiesandplay/u/toddler-activities.htm accessed 02/14/2012 p. 1 and 2

"A History of Public Education in the United States" by Deeptha Thattai, November13, 2018. url, www academic. edu/177440/A-history_ of_public_education

From Wikipedia, the free encyclopedia, Nov. 2, 2018 "History of education in the United states from the Seventeenth century to the early twenty-first century https//en, wikipedia.org/ wiki/ History- of education-the – United States

"Professional Administrators and Professional Teachers", by Bosman, Robert, and Charles A. Sloan, "The PERCEIVED CONCERNS OF ELEMENTARY SCHOOL PRINCIPALS AND ELEMENTARY SCHOOL TEACHERS TOWARD MAINSTREAMING 1979. ED. 193 795"

"Thomas Jefferson," Author, History.com. History URL, https://www.history.com Editors Website, History, URL, https://www.history.com/topics/us-presidents/ThomasJ efferson Access Date November 2, 2018, Publisher, A and E Television networks, Orginal Published Date, October29, 2009

Jack Jennings, Contributer Former President/CEO Center on Education Policy

03/28/2013/12:31pm E T I, Updated on 12/06/2017, URL, https//wwwhuffpost.com/entry/proportion-usstudents-b-2950948

very well mind, The 4 Stages of Cognitive Development, background and Key Concepts of Piaget's Theory, By Kendra Cherry, Medically reviewed by a board certified physician, Updated, May 20,2019, URL, https://www.verymind.com/piagets-stages-of-cognitive-development-2795457?print, p. 1-8

About the Author

Clynie Huggins was reared in a small rural community in Wharton, Texas, where she received her education in public schools. Her favorite hobbies were reading, spelling, writing, sewing, and playing the piano. Of course, she didn't realize then that she would become a teacher. At night, when everything was quiet, Clynie would get her composition book and write about the things that happened during the day, starting with the morning and ending at night. On the weekends, she would visit her grandparents, and they would always have interesting stories to tell of their childhoods. Clynie would listen, take notes, and add these notes to her composition book. These notes became real stories.

Clynie begin to dream of helping others with her talents of reading and writing. When she graduated from high school, she moved to Houston, Texas, where she enrolled in college. She graduated with a bachelor's degree in home economics and became a substitute teacher. She chose to teach in elementary schools, which she enjoyed. This inspired her to get a second bachelor's degree in elementary education and become a full-time teacher. Clynie also holds a master's degree in education administration. She has enjoyed helping kids to learn and work toward building a strong foundation in education which carries them through elementary, middle, high school, and college.

During Clynie's teaching career, she taught preschool through sixth grade but spent most of her years teaching second and third grades. Clynie felt that helping these students to master the skills at these grade levels were of great significance and played an important part in building a strong and efficient foundation in their education. Clynie loved teaching and helping kids to reach their greatest potential.

Clynie taught in elementary education for thirty-seven years. Now retired, her goals are to continue helping parents and their children in education through her non-profit organization, "The Clynie Huggins Foundation," public speaking and writing of educational books. Clynie wants to help parents learn and become knowledgeable in educating their children in the twenty-first century.

Clynie is married and has two adult children, and four grandchildren. Clynie helps to parent her youngest grandson. This experience enhances her parenting skills and makes her more knowledgeable in child development.

Printed in the United States
by Baker & Taylor Publisher Services